365

DREAMS

AND

INTERPRETATIONS

Email; tellaolayeri@gmail.com
Website www.tellaolayeri.com

US Contact

Ruth Jack

14 Milewood Road

Verbank

N.Y.12585

U.S.A. +19176428989

APPRECIATION

I give special appreciation to my wife MRS NGOZI OLAYERI for her assistance in ensuring that this book is published and our children that play around us to encourage us day and night.

Also, this manuscript wouldn't have seen the light of the day, if not for the spiritual encouragement I gathered from my father in the Lord, **Dr. D.K. OLUKOYA** who served as spiritual mirror that brightens my hope to explore my calling (Evangelism).

We shall all reap our blessings in heaven but the battle to make heaven is not over, until it is won.

GOOD NEWS!!!

My audiobook is now available. To get one go to acx.com and search **Tella Olayeri**.

Thanks.

PREVIOUS PUBLICATIONS OF THE AUTHOR

1. *Fire for Fire Prayer Book Part 1*
2. *Fire for Fire Prayer Book Part 2*
3. *My Marriage Shall Not Break*
4. *Prayer for Pregnant Women*
5. *Prayer for the Fruit of the Womb*
6. *Children Deliverance*
7. *Prayer for Youths and Teenagers*
8. *Prayer for Singles*
9. *Victory over Satanic House Part 1*
10. *Victory over Satanic House Part 2*
11. *I Shall Excel*
12. *Atomic Prayers that Destroy Witchcraft Powers and Silence Enemies*
13. *Goliath at the Gate of Marriage*
14. *Deliverance from Spirit of Dogs*
15. *Naked Warriors*
16. *Prayer Against Sex in the Dream*
17. *Strange Women! Leave My Husband Alone*
18. *Dangerous Prayer against Strange Women*
19. *630 Acidic Prayer Points*
20. *Prayer to Retain Job and Excel in Office*
21. *Warfare in the Office*
22. *Command the Year*
23. *Deliverance Prayer for First Born*
24. *800 Deliverance Prayer for First Born Part Two*
25. *Prayer for Good Health and Divine Healing*
26. *Prayer against Untimely Death.*

27. Dictionary of Dreams

28. Discover Gold and Build Wealth

29. My Head is not for Sale

30. 830 Prophecies for the Head

31. Atomic Prayers that Destroy Destiny Killers

32. Prayer after Dream

33. Prayer to Locate Helpers and helpers to locate you

34. Anointing for Eleventh Hour Help

35. 100% Confessions and Prophecies to Locate Helpers and helpers to locate you

36. Prayer to Remember Dreams

37. 1010 Dreams and interpretations

38. 650 Dreams and Interpretation

39. .1,000 Prayer Points for Children Breakthrough

40. I Am Not Alone

41. My Well of Honey shall not dry

42. Shake Heaven with Prayer and Praises

43. Deliverance Prayers for Middle Born Part One

44. 800 Deliverance Prayer Points for Middle Born Part Two

45. Deliverance Prayers for Last Born Part One

46. 800 Deliverance Prayer Points for Last Born Part Two

47. 365 Dreams and Interpretations

48. 700 Prayers to clear Unemployment Out of your Way

49. 777 Deliverance Prayers for Healing and Breakthrough

365 DREAMS AND INTERPRETATIONS

1. **IF YOU SEE BAD OR DAMAGED COMPUTER IN THE DREAM.** It means you have attitude that disrupts divine message from God. **Prayer.** My heart, unite with God in the name of Jesus.

2. **IF YOU SHARE MEAT IN SLAUGHTER HOUSE IN THE DREAM:** You are a witch that kills project at infancy or kill people in the spirit. **Prayer.** My soul, disengage from evil acts, in the name of Jesus.

3. **IF SINGLE AND SEE RIPE TWIN PLANTAIN SEED IN THE DREAM:** It means your partner to be is the right choice. **Prayer.** O Lord pour anointing of fertility upon my marriage, in the name of Jesus.

4. **IF SINGLE AND SEE TWIN PLANTAIN SEED; ONE GOOD AND THE OTHER SIDE BAD IN THE DREAM.** It means the person you propose to marry will not match you at all. **Prayer.** O Lord, locate me with the

bone of my bone and the flesh of my flesh, in the name of Jesus.

5. **IF YOU SAVE MONEY IN THE BANK IN THE DREAM.** It means fruitfulness and financial favour ahead. **Prayer.** Power of financial upliftment fall upon me, in the name of Jesus.

6. **IF YOU CARRY DEAD ANIMAL ON THE HEAD IN THE DREAM.** It means problems solved but dangerously reappear to consume you. **Prayer.** My destiny, receive total deliverance from evil arrows in the name of Jesus.

7. **IF YOU ARE DRAGGED FROM HIGHER SEAT TO OCCUPY LOWER SEAT IN THE DREAM.** It means arrow of the tail and demotion is fired at you. **Prayer.** I shall not be a subject of demotion, in the name of Jesus.

8. **IF YOU SAIL ON BUSINESS TRIP WITHOUT HINDERANCE IN THE DREAM.** It means financial explosion is on the way. **Prayer.** My breakthrough, appear by fire, in the name of Jesus.

9. **IF YOUR HAIR IS BUSHY AND UNKEPT IN THE DREAM.** It means

hindrance that brings rejection and poverty is on the way. **Prayer.** I reject by fire every spirit of poverty, in the name of Jesus.

10. **IF YOU RECEIVE PRECIOUS GIFTS IN EXCESS OF EXPECTATION IN THE DREAM.** It means outstanding breakthrough and favour shall locate you. **Prayer.** My heaven open wide and favour me, in the name of Jesus.

11. **IF PREGNANT AND FIND YOUR ABDOMEN UNCOVERED IN THE DREAM.** It means dark power is in operation against your safe delivery. **Prayer.** My life become too hot to handle by dark powers, in the name of Jesus.

12. **IF YOU DREAM TRAVELLING ABROAD IN THE DREAM.** It means high expectations, international connections, and or, physical manifestation of it. **Prayer.** My life you are a candidate for prosperity, in the name of Jesus.

13. **IF SOMEONE POUR ACID ON YOU IN THE DREAM.** It means imminent

danger from close associates. Prayer. Any power assign to torment my life die, in the name of Jesus.

14. **IF CAT SCARED AT YOU IN YOUR MATRIMONIAL BED IN THE DREAM**. It is a witchcraft marital attack against your home. **Prayer**. My marriage shall not bow to power of darkness, in the name of Jesus.

15. **IF YOU ARE BEHEADED IN THE DREAM.** It means sudden cut of dependable source of income or sudden death. **Prayer.** Every arrow of calamity fired against me backfire by fire, in the name of Jesus.

16. **IF YOU SEE BLACK BIRDS IN THE DREAM**. It means evil association against your life. **Prayer.** Every evil bird assign against me fall down and die, in the name of Jesus.

17. **IF YOU DREAM PAYING BILLS TO STRANGE FACES IN THE DREAM.** It means unexpected expenses and eventual loss of money in the offing. **Prayer**. My pocket, refuse satanic leakage, in the name of Jesus.

18. **IF YOU ARE GAINFULLY EMPLOYED BUT FOUND YOURSELFBEGGING FOR ALMS IN THE DREAM**. It means demotion and disgrace. **Prayer.** 0 Lord save me from destiny devourers, in the name of Jesus.

19. **IF STINKED BY BEES IN THE DREAM.** It is an attack from witchcraft powers. **Prayer.** Every power assign to sabotage my plan receive total disgrace, in the name of Jesus.

20. **IF YOU EAT WITH ANTI CHRIST FOLLOWERS IN THE DREAM.** It means strong warning against spiritual diversion. **Prayer.** Spiritual failure shall not be my portion, in the name of Jesus.

21. **IF YOU SIT ON A BENCH AND BITTEN BYINSECTS IN THE DREAM.** It is a strong warning not to over relax as there may be attack in the offing. **Prayer.** 1 shall not sleep off for enemies to conquer, in the name of Jesus.

22. **IF YOU HAVE TWO WIVES IN THE DREAM.** It means spiritual wife or strange women are firing evil arrow at

you. **Prayer**. My spirit, soul and body reject polygamy in the name of Jesus.

23. **IF ROBBED IN BANK PREMISES IN THE DREAM.** It means failure at point of harvest. **Prayer**. I shall reap the sweat of my labour, in the name of Jesus.

24. **IF YOU FIND IT DIFFICUFLT TO LEAVE FLOOR LEVEL TO UPPER LEVEL OF YOUR CHOICE IN THE DREAM**. It means physical frustration and failure. **Prayer**. My soul shall not trade with failure, in the name of Jesus.

25. **IF YOUR BASIN OF WATER IS STOLEN IN THE DREAM.** It means loss of anointing and blessings that may affect you. **Prayer.** Every step taken by evil powers to rob me of my anointing die, in the name of Jesus.

26. **WHEN TURNED BACK IN A QUEU WHERE THINGS ARE SHARED IN THE DREAM.** It means your effort shall meet brick wall of rejection in the physical. **Prayer.** Every mountain assign against my life scatter, in the name of Jesus.

27. **IF SINGLE AND YOU SEE YOURSELF PLAYING WITH BULL**

IN THE DREAM. It means strong warning in respect of whom you are proposing at the moment. **Prayer.** 0 Lord save me from marrying wrong partner in life, in the name of Jesus.

28. **IF OFFERED BRIGHT AND COLOURFUL BUTTONS IN THE DREAM.** It means good connections that bring wealth. **Prayer.** O Lord, connect me with people at the right time, in the name of Jesus.

29. **IF YOU SEE EVIL ANIMAL CAGED IN THE DREAM.** It means evil powers assigned against you have been caged. **Prayer.** Holy Ghost Power paralyze evil power assign against me, in the name of Jesus.

30. **IF YOU ARE BURIED IN THE DREAM.** It means sudden death or high problem you cannot solve ordinarily. **Prayer.** I release my soul from evil arrows, in the name of Jesus.

31. **IF YOU JOYFULLY RECEIVE CABLEGRAM MESSAGE IN THE DREAM.** It means news of joy will soon be heard by you. **Prayer.** My days of joy

shall not change to sorrow, in the name of Jesus.

32. **IF YOU SEE BUTTERFLY FEEDING ON FLOWERS IN THE DREAM.** It means joy and pleasantry. **Prayer.** O Lord open new doors of blessings to me, in the name of Jesus.

33. **IF YOU LICK BUTTER IN THE DREAM.** It means open door of prosperity is in the offing **Prayer.** My days of prosperity appear now, in the name of Jesus.

34. **IF BOARD A CALM SAILING SHIP IN THE DREAM.** It means long term expectation that bring fruitfulness. **Prayer.** My hope of greatness shall be fulfilled in the name of Jesus.

35. **IF DISCHARGED AND AQUITED BEFORE A LAW COURT IN THE DREAM.** It means victory over satanic powers delegated against your life. **Prayer.** I shall be a winner not a loser in the name of Jesus.

36. **IF YOU BOARD AIRCRAFT TO A PROPOSED DESTINATION IN THE DREAM.** Expect speedy answer to your breakthrough **Prayer.** O Lord lift me to

my place of fulfillment in the name of Jesus.

37. **IF YOU SEE FARM VEGETATION EATEN BY PEST IN THE DREAM.** It means failure and cry over your labour. **Prayer.** I shall not be double crossed by evil powers in the name of Jesus.

38. **IF YOU SEE JET BOMBER BOMBING A CITY IN THE DREAM.** It means high confusion or war in the offing. **Prayer.** Power of peace, take over my environment in the name of Jesus.

39. **IF YOU ENCOUNTER STUBBORN OPPOSITION IN THE DREAM.** It means evil gang up against you is in the offing. **Prayer.** Holy Ghost Fire, scatter every evil gang up against me in the name of Jesus.

40. **IF YOU ARE DRAGGED OUT OF A CONGREGATION IN THE DREAM.** It means rejection and demotion in life. **Prayer.** Oppositions against my life seize by fire in the name of Jesus.

41. **IF YOU ARE FORCED TO MATCH THROUGH BROKEN BOTTLES IN THE DREAM.** It means power of delay

and failure is assign against you **Prayer**. Power of delay and failure in my life die, in the name of Jesus.

42. **IF YOU LOSE BRIEFCASE TO ROBBERS IN THE DREAM.** It means spiritual robbers assigned to rob you of your prospects in life are in operation. **Prayer**. Thou spirit robbers-assigned to empty my joy die in the name of Jesus.

43. **IF YOU CROSS A BROKEN DOWN BRIDGE IN THE DREAM.** It means haste in solving problems to get answer. **Prayer**. Spirit of double standard in my life die, in the name of Jesus.

44. **IF YOU CLEAR YOUR FARMLAND WITH BLUNT CUTLASS IN THE DREAM.** It means much labour with little harvest. **Prayer**. O Lord, sharpen my ideas for greater harvest, in the name of Jesus.

45. **IF YOU HOLD NEW BRIEFCASE IN THE DREAM.** It means new opportunities and subsequent breakthrough in life. **Prayer**. Opportunities to excel in life locate me by fire in the name of Jesus.

46. **IF YOUR HOUSE IS FULL OF BROKEN WALLS IN THE DREAM.** It means your plans have filtered to the hands of enemies and are ready to attack. **Prayer.** My joy shall not be cut short by powers of darkness in the name of Jesus.

47. **IF YOU BAKE BREAD IN THE DREAM.** It means resourcefulness and security in life. **Prayer.** Power to excel fall upon me, in the name of Jesus.

48. **IF YOU SEE BARRICADES ON YOUR WAY IN THE DREAM.** It means delay in progress and breakthrough. **Prayer.** Powers, assign to delay me die, in the name of Jesus.

49. **IF YOU BATH IN AN OPEN SPACE IN THE DREAM.** It means you have taken a step that may bring disgrace into your life **Prayer.** Every arrow of disgrace fired against my life backfire by fire in the name of Jesus.

50. **IF YOU RECEIVE GIFT OF HONOUR IN THE DREAM.** It means open door to prosperity and joy is on the way. **Prayer.** O Lord let me see favour of men and women, in the name of Jesus.

51. **IF YOU SEE ALLIGATOR IN THE DREAM.** It means warning in respect of business or career you want to pursue. **Prayer.** Thou storm of destruction against my life seize by fire, in the name of Jesus.

52. **IF OVERPOWERED IN A DUEL IN THE DREAM.** It means failure in business and career pursuits. **Pray.** I shall be a winner not a loser in the name of Jesus.

53. **IF PURSUED BUT COULD NOT BE ARRESTED IN THE DREAM** It means victory over stubborn pursuers. **Prayer.** Every power delegated against me die, in the name of Jesus.

54. **IF COVENIENTLY SITED IN AN ARMCHAIR IN THE DREAM.** It means exalted position awaits you. **Prayer.** O Lord, support me from all direction.

55. **IF YOU ARE ANGRY IN THE DREAM.** It means misunderstanding and confusion may practically arise soonest. **Prayer.** Powers that open gate of disorder in people's life die, in the name Jesus.

56. **IF YOU SEE RIPE FRUITS IN THE DREAM**. It means favourable time of harvest of your labour is at hand: **Prayer**. Joy and happiness of mind locate me by fire in the name of Jesus.

57. **IF YOU PREACH IN THE CHURCH ALTAR IN THE DREAM**. It means God's calling. **Prayer.** Power to serve God beyond human understanding fall upon me, in the name of Jesus.

58. **IF YOU SEE ANCHOR IN THE DREAM.** It means arrow of stagnancy is fired against you. **Prayer**. Every arrow of stagnancy fired against my life backfire by fire, in the name of Jesus.

59. **IF YOUR TWO ARMS ARE CHOPED OFF IN THE DREAM**: It means slow progress and failure in whatever you lay hand upon. **Prayer.** My hand reject evil summon, in the name of Jesus.

60. **IF AMBUSH IS LAID AGAINST YOU IN THE DREAM.** It means secret plans are on the way against your success **Prayer**. O Lord, save me from the hands of unfriendly friends in the name of Jesus.

61. **IF YOU SAIL IN COOL AND CALM WEATHER IN THE DREAM.** It means profitable venture or career in the offing. **Prayer.** O Lord, pour anointing of financial breakthrough upon my life, in the name of Jesus.

62. **IF YOU TRAVEL IN A BOAT AND IT SUDDENLY SINK IN THE DREAM.** It means evil arrow is fired against your marriage, career or calling **prayer**. O Lord, save me from the wicked arrow of the enemy.

63. **IF YOU READ BUT COULD NOT UNDERSTAND IN THE DREAM.** It means problem that need deep meaning will soon be presented to you for solution. **Prayer.** Wisdom that is above understanding fall upon me in the name of Jesus.

64. **IF YOU SEE BOIL ON YOUR FOREHEAD IN The DREAM.** It means sickness or arrow of infirmity. **Prayer.** O Lord, disgrace every arrows of sickness fired against me, in the name of Jesus.

65. **IF YOU SEE SEEDS BOILED IN THE DREAM.** It means your seed of

life is under attack. **Prayer**. O Lord, save me from powers assign to destroy my joy, in the name of Jesus.

66. **IF YOU ARE IN A BOAT FAR IN THE DEEP SEA WITHOUT ENDING IN THE DREAM.** It means marine connection. **Prayer**. I break myself loose from marine power, in the name of Jesus.

67. **IF YOU FIRE ARROW AND MISS THE TARGET IN THE DREAM.** It means failure concerning ventures ahead of you. **Prayer**. Every master plan of the enemy against my life scatter by fire in the name of Jesus.

68. **IF YOU SEE SICK BABIES IN THE DREAM.** It means bad health of new ventures in your hand. **Prayer**. O Lord, direct me rightly in my venture and career in the name of Jesus.

69. **IF YOU SHARPEN CUTLASS IN THE DREAM.** It means you are presently taking bold step to victory in your career or business. **Prayer**. Power that open great doors of victory and breakthroughs fall upon me.

70. **IF YOU LEAVE SMALLER CAR AND OCCUPY BIGGER ONE IN THE DREAM.** 1t means promotion and success. **Prayer.** My destiny receive revival of breakthrough in the name of Jesus.

71. **IF YOU DREAM AND SEE YOUR HUSBAND WORKING HARD WITH AXE IN THE DREAM.** It means hard labour before he can feed. **Prayer.** O Lord open doors of prosperity unto my spouse in the name of Jesus.

72. **IF YOU DREAM OF DULL WEATHER.** It means conspiracy that brings financial embargo in the offing. **Prayer.** Every evil cloud assign against my success disappear in the name of Jesus.

73. **IF YOU SEE CLEAR AND BRIGHT WHEATHER IN THE DREAM**: It means open door to success. **Prayer.** Doors of blessings open unto my life, in the name of Jesus.

74. **IF MARRIED BUT WAS SINGLE IN THE DREAM:** It is a signal of marital turbulence. **Prayer.** My marriage shall not experience evil arrow, in the name of Jesus.

75. **IF YOU DREAM OF A BOOK SHELF FULLY STOCKED.** It means success in academics and writing. **Prayer.** O Lord, bless my destiny with academic success, in the name of Jesus.

76. **IF YOU RECEIVE BAD BREAD IN THE DREAM.** It means ill-luck and likely introduction of sickness into your body. **Prayer.** I shall live but not die, in the name of Jesus.

77. **IF YOU SEE GREEN-FLOURISHING TREE IN THE DREAM.** It means better connection and prosperity through important personalities. **Prayer.** O Lord let my helpers see and help me in the name of Jesus.

78. **IF YOU HOLD A CONTAINER WITH JOY IN THE DREAM:** It means people will rally round you but be aware of fake friends **Prayer**. I shall not be a candidate of mockery in the name of Jesus.

79. **IF YOU WIN IN A BOXING COMPETITION IN THE DREAM.** It means fruitful success after hard work. **Prayer**. O Lord, crown my labour with success in the name of Jesus.

80. **IF YOUR VEHICLE SUDDENLY BREAK DOWN IN THE DREAM.** It means satanic delay in life. **Prayer**. Thou vehicle of my destiny receive divine anointing, in the name of Jesus.

81. **IF YOU SEE SEALED BOTTLE IN THE DREAM.** It means your opportunity is sealed spiritually. **Prayer.** Any wicked power assign against my life die, in the name of Jesus.

82. **IF YOU TAKE BACK DOOR OF THE HOUSE INSTEAD OF FRONT**

DOOR IN THE DREAM. It means doing wrong thing at the right time. **Prayer.** Misplaced priorities in my life seize by fire, in the name of Jesus.

83. **IF YOU TAKE WRONG ROUTE IN THE DREAM.** It means arrow of confusion and stagnancy is fired against you. **Prayer.** I shall not fail in life in the name of Jesus.

84. **IF YOU PLAY DRAFT OR LUDO IN THE DREAM.** It means preoccupation of mind with vain things. **Prayer.** I marry my life to fruitfulness and not poverty, in the name of Jesus.

85. **IF YOU SEE BALOON IN THE DREAM.** It means short time joy, **Prayer.** O Lord, occupy my life with lasting laughter, in the name of Jesus.

86. **IF ELECTROCUTED IN THE DREAM.** It means imminent danger ahead or arrow of death is fired against you. **Prayer.** Thou coffin prepared for

me in the spirit catch fire, in the name of Jesus.

87. **IF YOU EAT BAD BANANA IN THE MIDST OF GOOD ONES IN THE DREAM.** It means denial of oneself of goodness because of stubbornness and refusal to take advice. **Prayer.** Thou stubborn spirit in me die, in the name of Jesus.

88. **IF YOU ARE ON THE WINNING SIDE OF A FOOTBALL COMPETITION IN THE DREAM.** It means victory and excitements are in the offing. **Prayer**. O Lord materialize my goodness now, in the name of Jesus.

89. **IF YOU SEE AN INJURED WHITE BIRD IN THE DREAM.** It is a sign of polluted spiritual life. **Prayer.** Powers that drag one from God in my life die, in the name of Jesus.

90. **IF YOU CATCH BIRDS WITH SMILES IN THE DREAM.** It means open door to breakthrough and

evangelism. **Prayer**. Power to raise candidates of heaven fall upon me, in the name of Jesus.

91. **IF ATTEND INTERVIEW AND LOST YOUR HANDBAG ALONG THE WAY IN THE DREAM.** It means failure to excel in life. **Prayer.** Spirit of delay in my life die in the name of Jesus.

92. **IF OFFERED SALT MIXED WITH SAND IN THE DREAM.** It means powers that pollute joy are in the offing. **Prayer.** My success shall not hit the rock, in the name of Jesus.

93. **IF YOU EXPERIENCE BITTER TASTE IN THE DREAM.** It means evil discussion and approach to matters. **Prayer.** Tongue that bring disaster to life seize by fire, in the name of Jesus.

94. **IF PRESENTED WITH EMPTY NEST IN THE DREAM.** It means poor turnout in business or career. **Prayer**. My plans to fruitfulness shall not be aborted, in the name of Jesus.

95. **IF YOU JOYFULLY MARK YOUR BIRTHDAY IN THE DREAM.** It means joy and progress in life. **Prayer.** O Lord, make my days on earth a remarkable one in the name of Jesus.

96. **IF YOU LICK BITTER THING IN THE DREAM.** It means self-affliction. **Prayer.** Affliction, afflictions in my life die in the name of Jesus.

97. **IF YOU SEE CAKE IN THE DREAM.** It means joy and fruitfulness in life. **Prayer.** My joy shall know no boundary, in the name of Jesus.

98. **IF YOU MARK A PARTICULAR DATE IN THE CALENDAR IN THE DREAM.** It means a particular day of importance is at hand. **Prayer.** My day of joy appear by fire, in the name of Jesus.

99. **IF YOU KEEP FILES IN THE DREAM.** It means you shall serve in a position of trust. **Prayer.** My life, surrender to powers of glory and fulfillment, in the name of Jesus.

100. **IF YOU SEE WELL-FED CALF IN THE DREAM.** It means success in

pursuits the offing. **Prayer.** Dumbfounding breakthrough locate me by fire in the name of Jesus.

101. **IF BLACKMAILED IN THE DREAM.** It means gathering cloud of conspiracy and rejection is in the offing. **Prayer.** Any power assign to pull me down die by fire in the name of Jesus.

102. **IF YOU ARE GIVEN ARROW IN THE DREAM.** It means you shall be a person of authority in real life. **Prayer.** O Lord, manifest the leadership in me now in the name of Jesus.

103. **IF YOU SEE BLACKSMITH ON DUTY IN THE DREAM.** It means your efforts shall soon experience harvest in real life. **Prayer.** O Lord, empower me with fruitful harvest in the name of Jesus.

104. **IF YOU BLEED IN THE DREAM.** It means loss of virtue in the physical. **Prayer.** O Lord, save me from arrows of darkness, in the name of Jesus.

105. **IF YOU SEE STAIN ALL OVER YOUR BODY IN THE DREAM.** It means mark of rejection that breeds poverty. **Prayer.** Blood of Jesus cleanse me of evil marks in the name of Jesus.

106. **IF YOU LOSE YOUR TEETH IN THE DREAM.** It means wicked attacks on your strength. **Prayer.** Thou power assign to promote shame in my life die in the name of Jesus.

107. **IF YOU EXCHANGE BLOWS WITH SOMEONE IN THE DREAM.** It means climate of confusion and distraction from progress is in the offing. **Prayer.** Spirit of greatness locate me by fire in the name of Jesus.

108. **IF YOU SUCCESSFULLY CLIMB A PALM TREE WITH FRUITS IN THE DREAM.** It means success and fruitfulness in your venture. **Prayer.** O Lord bless the works of my hand in the name of Jesus.

109. **IF YOU ARE IN A ROTTEN COCOA FARM IN THE DREAM.** It means shattered hope in business. **Prayer.** I shall not swim in poverty in the name of Jesus.

110. **IF SITTED ON A CHAIR WITH INCOMPLETE LEGS IN THE DREAM.** It means your plan at hand shall meet hindrance and delay. **Prayer.**

O Lord, execute my good plans for me in the name of Jesus.

111. **IF YOU SEE DOVE IN THE DREAM.** It means peace, spiritual strength and satisfaction. **Prayer.** Holy Spirit Divine, locate my life in the name of Jesus.

112. **IF YOU ARE DROWNED IN A RIVER IN THE DREAM.** It means danger; unfulfilled promise and downward trend in business or career making. **Prayer** Blessing that cannot be covered by power of darkness be my portion, in the name of Jesus.

113. **IF YOU SEE EROSION IN THE DREAM.** It means physical hindrance in your life may soon disappear. **Prayer.** My life, arise and shine in the name of Jesus.

114. **IF YOU FALL IN THE DREAM.** It means relegation in status or downward trend in business. **Prayer.** My life, arise and shine in the name of Jesus.

115. **IF YOU SEE FLIES IN THE DREAM.** It is a symbol of failure and invalid venture. **Prayer.** Power that

destroy investment die, in the name of Jesus.

116. **IF YOU STRIKE YOUR LEG ON HARD OBJECT IN THE DREAM.** It means negative expectation that may bring ill-luck in life is in the offing. **Prayer.** Every symptom of ill-luck in my life die in the name of Jesus.

117. **IF YOU HOLD BROKEN LANTERN IN THE DREAM.** It means unfulfill hope and eventual loss in business. **Prayer.** O Lord, guide my steps to life fulfillment in the name of Jesus.

118. **IF YOU RIDE BICYCLE OR MOTOR BYKE SMOOTHTLY IN THE DREAM.** It means two yielding business is open to you. **Prayer.** Fruitful expectation in my life be fulfilled in the name of Jesus.

119. **IF YOU URINATE BLOOD IN THE DREAM**. It means danger of great magnitude. **Prayer.** I release my soul from danger in the name of Jesus.

120. **IF YOU SEE WATER FALLS IN THE DREAM.** It means abundant blessing. **Prayer.** Blessing that cannot be

quantify fall upon me in the name of Jesus.

121. **IF YOU DREAM OF MOUSE UNDERNEATH YOUR BED.** It means satanic agent of destruction is on guide in your house. **Prayer.** Every agent of darkness assign against my life die, in the name of Jesus.

122. **IF YOU ARE IN A TATTERED DRESS TO AN INTERVIEW IN THE DREAM.** It means spirit of rejection and failure is after you. **Prayer.** My life, reject failure in the name of Jesus.

123. **IF YOUR CAR IS PACKED ON A TREE IN THE DREAM.** It means it has been assigned for satanic meeting in the spirit. **Prayer.** My property, be a fire in the hand of the enemy.

124. **IF OFFERED KNOT IN THE DREAM.** It connotes suicide spirit. **Prayer.** Spirit of untimely death in my life die in the name of Jesus.

125. **IF YOU WALK WITH EASE ON A NEWROAD IN THE DREAM.** It means new expectation awaits you soonest. **Prayer.** I claim my victory by fire in the name of Jesus.

126. **IF YOU DREAM AND IT IS ALWAYS ERASED.** It is satanic attack. **Prayer.** Thou dream eraser in my life die in the name of Jesus.

127. **IF YOU DREAM POSTING LETTER.** It means news of pleasure and goodness in the offing. **Prayer.** Heavenly joy, locate me by fire in the name of Jesus.

128. **If YOU EXPERIENCE PHONE FAILURE IN THE DREAM.** It signifies attack against your communication with God. **Prayer.** My prayer life resurrect by fire in the name of Jesus.

129. **IF YOUR PROPERTY IS BURGLED IN THE DREAM.** It is an attack of household wickedness that may lead to poverty. **Prayer.** Every conspiracy of household wickedness against me, scatter by fire in the name of Jesus.

130. **IF YOU RECEIVE FLOWER IN THE DREAM.** It means joy and or, marital proposal ahead. **Prayer.** Divine winds of joy locate me by fire in the name of Jesus.

131. **IF YOU PLANT SEED IN THE DREAM.** It means spirit of evangelism, church planting and miracles ahead. **Prayer.** O Lord, fertilize the seed of God in me in the name of Jesus.

132. **IF YOU ARE HUNGRY AND THIRSTY IN THE DREAM.** It connotes spirit of discomfort and dissatisfaction. **Prayer.** My spirit, receive anointing of comfort in the name of Jesus.

133. **IF YOU KILL VULTURE IN THE DREAM.** It means power over death and hell. **Prayer.** Every assignment of death against my life, scatter in the name of Jesus.

134. **IF YOU VOMIT SNAILS IN THE DREAM.** It means victory over power of sluggishness and delay in life. **Prayer.** I claim divine victory over arrows of failure in the name of Jesus.

135. **IF YOU WALK OUT OF CEMETARY IN THE DREAM.** It means you are delivered of sudden death. **Prayer.** Power that open doors of prosperity appear in my life in the name of Jesus.

136. **IF YOU WATCH FOOTBALL MATCH IN THE DREAM.** It means excitement and joy. **Prayer.** I paralyze any power standing against my joy, in the name of Jesus.

137. **IF YOU ARE IN ARMY UNIFORM IN THE DREAM.** It signifies spiritual upliftment and progress. **Prayer.** Power to fight my battle to victory, be my portion in the name of Jesus.

138. **IF YOU FIND YOUR LOST CAP IN THE DREAM.** It means overcoming plans of disgrace against you. **Prayer.** Every conspiracy against my life scatter in the name of Jesus.

139. **IF COW SWALLOW YOUR DOCUMENT IN THE DREAM.** It is a serious attack against your progress in life, **Prayer.** Any satanic, animal assign against my progress die, in the name of Jesus.

140. **IF YOUR CLOTH BURN IN THE DREAM.** It means arrow of destruction and affliction is fired against you. **Prayer:** I fire back every arrow of affliction fired against me, in the name of Jesus.

141. **IF YOU ARE SERVED RED SUBSTANCE IN THE DREAM**. It means initiation or participation in witchcraft drink of blood. **Prayer.** My soul, reject satanic activities in the name of Jesus.

142. **IF YOU DIG BURRIED POT IN THE DREAM.** This is a victorious dream of exhuming your buried potentials. **Prayer.** Power to locate my breakthrough fall upon me, in the name of Jesus.

143. **IF YOU SCORE PASS MARK IN AN INTERVIEW IN THE DREAM.** It means you shall experience promotion and breakthrough in life. **Prayer.** I shall excel and not fail in life, in the name of Jesus.

144. **IF OFFERED OR SAW DEAD SEEDS IN THE DREAM**. It is a serious dead blow against your finances, ministry or career. **Prayer.** Any good thing dead that is dead in my life come alive by the power in the blood of Jesus.

145. **IF YOU ARE HOSPITALISED IN THE DREAM**. It is a warning of an impending health hazard in the offing.

Prayer. O Lord incubates my family and me with your power in the name of Jesus.

146. **IF YOU PREACH IN THE DREAM.** It is a sign of calling. **Prayer.** O Lord show me the ministry I am called to serve in the name of Jesus.

147. **IF YOU HAVE HAND SHAKE WITH INFLUENTIAL PEOPLE IN THE DREAM.** It means elevation and promotion shall locate you. **Prayer.** O Lord open my door of promotion in the name of Jesus.

148. **IF YOU SUCCESSFULLY CROSS AN OCEAN IN THE DREAM.** It means dividend of joy and breakthrough shall locate you as you overcome long term storm in life. **Prayer.** My liberty and progress appear by fire in the name of Jesus.

149. **IF YOU SEPERATE TWO PEOPLE FIGHTING IN THE DREAM.** It means you shall be of help to mediate for people. **Prayer.** Wisdom that surpasses human understanding fall upon me in the name of Jesus.

150. **WHEN YOU SEE YOURSELF BREAKING YOUR FAMILY**

SHRINE IN THE DREAM. It means victory over evil foundation. **Prayer.** Thou fire of God heal the foundation of my family in the name of Jesus.

151. **IF YOU EXPERIENCE WAVES AGAINST YOUR BOAT IN THE DREAM.** It means your career or business shall experience strong opposition. **Prayer.** My God overcome every opposition against me in the name of Jesus.

152. **IF YOU ARE IN AN EVIL FOREST IN THE DREAM.** It symbolizes strange attack on the way. **Prayer.** My life shall not be candidate of wicked plots in the name of Jesus.

153. **IF YOUR KEYS ARE STOLEN IN THE DREAM.** It means loss of authority and power to excel in life. **Prayer.** I recover my lost glory in the name of Jesus.

154. **IF YOU FIND YOURSELF PRAYING IN THE CHURCH.** It is a good omen signifying progress and divine protection. **Prayer.** O Lord, lay your hand of success upon me in the name of Jesus.

155. **IF FLOGGED IN THE DREAM.** It means disgrace and satanic attack upon your dignity. **Prayer.** Any sponsored disgrace and attack against me scatter by fire in the name of Jesus.

156. **IF YOU CARRY CROSS IN THE DREAM.** It means taking care of pains and needs of people around you. **Prayer.** Power to give sacrificial help to people fall upon me in the name of Jesus.

157. **IF YOU SEE COLLAPSE BUILDING IN THE DREAM.** It is a sign of impending danger and frustration against your ministry, family or close ones. **Prayer.** I nullify every impending danger on my way in the name of Jesus.

158. **IF YOU PUT DOWN LOAD FROM YOUR HEAD IN THE DREAM.** It is a sign of victory over evil load and frustration. **Prayer.** My destiny, receive freedom by fire in the name of Jesus.

159. **IF YOU SEE TORTOISE IN THE DREAM.** It means spirit of delay and cunning people are around you. **Prayer.** O Lord, reveal unto me every unfriendly friend around me in the name of Jesus.

160. **IF YOU SEE WOMAN WITH FISH TAIL IN THE DREAM.** It is a marine connection. **Prayer.** I break every relationship I have with marine powers in the name of Jesus.

161. **IF OFFERED FAKE CURRENCY IN THE DREAM.** It means financial difficulties and likely attacks from dupers. **Prayer.** O Lord create gap between me and powers that create sorrow.

162. **IF YOU ARE OFFERED GOOD TOUCH LIGHT IN THE DREAM.** It means divine direction with purpose will soon come your way. **Prayer.** Light of purpose locate me by fire in the name of Jesus.

163. **IF YOU ARE OFFERED SALT IN THE DREAM.** It connotes purity, good health and joy on the way. **Prayer.** I shall be a salt of life in the name of Jesus.

164. **IF URINE IS POURED ON YOU IN THE DREAM.** It is an attack of rejection and frustration. **Prayer.** Blood of Jesus wash me clean of wicked pollution in the name of Jesus.

TELLA OLAYERI

165. **IF YOU ARE OFFERED CERTIFICATE OF MERIT IN THE DREAM.** It means that soonest physical promotion and joy shall locate you. **Prayer.** My destiny move forward by fire in the name of Jesus.

166. **IF YOU CULTIVATE NEW FARMLAND IN THE DREAM.** It means new opportunities will soon appear in your life. **Prayer.** Ability to know my opportunities as they appear fall upon me in the name of Jesus.

167. **IF YOU ARE GIVEN SEASON INVITATION CARD IN THE DREAM.** It means good news is in the offing. **Prayer.** News that bring promotion be my portion in the name of Jesus.

168. **IF YOU SEE AN OWL ON YOUR BED IN THE DREAM.** It signifies bad health that may lead to sudden death. **Prayer.** I reject every form of sickness in the name of Jesus.

169. **IF YOU ARE OFFERED CLEAN SATCHET WATER IN THE DREAM.** It means answer to thirst for business, career or job is in the offing.

Prayer. O Lord, empower me to take steps that lead to breakthrough in life in the name of Jesus.

170. **IF A LETTER IS HANDED TO YOU AND YOUBURST INTO TEARS IN THE DREAM.** It means bad news is in the offing. **Prayer.** I cancel every form of bad news awaiting me in the name of Jesus.

171. **IF YOUR DOOR IS UNDER LOCK AND KEY IN THE DREAM.** It means disappointment, ill-luck emanating from evil attack. **Prayer.** My source of breakthrough shall not be blocked by evil padlock in the name of Jesus.

172. **IF YOU EXCHANGE GIFT IN THE DREAM.** It means warm atmosphere with neighbors depending on what you receive as gift. **Prayer.** Laughter that promotes peace of mind locate me by fire in the name of Jesus.

173. **IF FLOOD SUDDENLY STOP IN THE DREAM.** It means serious problem facing you shall soon be over. **Prayer.** Thou flood of poverty fashioned against my life disappear in the name of Jesus.

174. **IF YOU ROMANCE WITH STRANGE PERSON IN THE DREAM.** It means spirit spouse is in your affair. **Prayer.** I divorce every spirit husband/wife in my life in the name of Jesus.

175. **IF A STRANGE PERSON DRIVES YOU IN THE DREAM.** It means evil diversion that leads to failure. **Prayer.** Thou strange power delegated against me die in the name of Jesus.

176. **IF YOU DREAM OF RESTING ON A BROKEN CHAIR.** It means you are surrounded by unreliable supporters or ill-luck in office. **Prayer.** Every unfriendly friend in my life be exposed and be defeated in the name of Jesus.

177. **IF YOU CRY OVER THE DEATH OF A CHILD IN THE DREAM.** It means a new venture you want to lay hand upon may fail. It may also mean physical death as well. **Prayer.** I shall prevail in life in the name of Jesus.

178. **IF YOUR HOUSE OVERGROW WITH WEED IN THE DREAM.** It means hindrance and problems that must be solved are in the offing. **Prayer.**

Ability to tackle problems as they arise fall upon me in the name of Jesus.

179. **IF YOU HOLD DEAD DOVE IN YOUR HAND IN THE DREAM.** It means your handwork is bringing problem instead of peace. **Prayer.** I shall not walk under the shadow of problem in the name of Jesus.

180. **IF YOU WALK INSIDE FEACES IN THE DREAM.** It means spirit of uncleanness that leads to rejection in life is ravaging your life. **Prayer.** Father Lord save me from evil companion.

181. **IF YOU LOST SWORD IN THE DREAM.** It means loss of power and authority in the physical is in the offing. **Prayer.** Power that strengthen one against evil forces fall upon me in the name of Jesus.

182. **IF YOUR BODY IS FULL OF SORE IN THE DREAM**. It means arrow of sickness. **Prayer.** Fire of God; protect me twenty four hours daily in the name of Jesus.

183. **IF YOU RECEIVE LOAF OF BREAD IN THE DREAM.** It means divine provision of needs. **Prayer**. My blessing

shall not pass me by in the name of Jesus.

184. **IF YOU ESCAPE FROM PIT THROUGH A HELPING HAND IN THE DREAM.** This signifies victory and deliverance from evil cage. **Prayer.** Angels of God save me from evil plots in the name of Jesus.

185. **IF YOU ARE SERVED QUIT NOTICE IN THE DREAM.** It is a signal of strong quarrel and misunderstanding in the offing. **Prayer.** Powers that sponsor sorrow shall not locate me in the name of Jesus.

186. **IF YOUR CLOTH STAIN IN THE DREAM.** It portrays evil mark upon your personality. **Prayer.** My garment, turn to fire in the hand of my enemies in the name of Jesus.

187. **IF YOUR SHOE IS LOST IN THE DREAM.** It means marital problem in the physical. **Prayer.** My marriage shall not break in the name of Jesus.

188. **IF YOU DREAM YOUR SPOUSE IS MISSING IN THE DREAM.** It foretells satanic attack against your marriage and household. **Prayer.** O

Lord, save my marriage from calamity in the name of Jesus.

189. **IF YOU FIGHT IN A FOOTBALL MATCH IN THE DREAM.** It means evil arrow has been fired against your joy and excitement. **Prayer.** Every power assign to terminate joy in my life die in the name of Jesus.

190. **IF YOU ARE SERVED GLASS PLATE IN THE DREAM.** It signifies upliftment and promotion in the offing. **Prayer.** My life, receive divine upliftment and promotion in the name of Jesus.

191. **IF YOU DREAM OF MONSTER CHASING YOU IN THE DREAM.** It means power of local wickedness is after your life. **Prayer.** Every power of local wickedness after my life summersault and die in the name of Jesus.

192. **IF YOU ARE HANDCUFFED IN THE DREAM**. It means serious problem that leads to spiritual captivity, delay and stagnancy in real life. **Prayer.** O Lord save me from cage of wickedness in the name of Jesus.

193. **IF CROWNED IN THE SEA IN THE DREAM.** It means marine initiation. **Prayer.** I break myself loose from marine manipulation in the name of Jesus.

194. **IF YOU CLIMB A DEAD TREE IN THE DREAM.** It means laying claim on fruitless efforts that leads to failure and poverty. **Prayer.** My effort shall not be in vain in the name of Jesus.

195. **IF YOU TRADE WITH THE DEAD IN THE DREAM.** It means your spirit is connected to dead relatives or friends. **Prayer.** I release my spirit from power of the dead in the name of Jesus.

196. **IF YOU DREAM OF HOLE IN THE POCKET.** It means satanic attack on your finance, status and or loss in business. **Prayer.** O Lord, save me from evil agenda of the enemy in the name of Jesus.

197. **IF COVERED WITH THICK DARKNESS IN THE DREAM.** It means arrow of confusion, delay and poverty is fired against you. **Prayer.** Every arrow of confusion fired against my life backfire in the name of Jesus.

198. **IF YOU ARE IN A CINEMA HALL IN THE DREAM.** It means diversion of seriousness from things of God. **Prayer.** My faith shall not shake in things of God in the name of Jesus.

199. **IF YOU SEE BOIL ALL OVER YOUR BODY IN THE DREAM.** It means sickness that brings discomfort is in the offing. **Prayer.** My life is not for sickness, therefore-arrow of sickness die, in the name of Jesus.

200. **IF SOLDIERS OVERTAKE YOUR HOUSE IN THE DREAM.** It means satanic attack that causes panic and loss are in the offing. **Prayer.** Every plan of the enemy against my household scatter in the name of Jesus.

201. **IF YOU TEACH CHILDREN IN THE DREAM.** It means your calling is for children upliftment. **Prayer.** My calling and career manifest by fire in the name of Jesus.

202. **IF YOU PULL BLACK CLOTH IN YOUR BODY IN THE DREAM.** It means victory over untimely death. **Prayer.** I shall not be a casualty in the hand of the enemy.

203. **IF YOU ADDRESS A CROWD IN A BACONY IN THE DREAM.** It is a sign of leadership in the offing. **Prayer**. My destiny, occupy rightful position by fire in the name of Jesus.

204. **IF A STRANGE PERSON COLLECTS YOUR GIFT FROM YOU IN THE DREAM.** It means loss of spiritual gift in the physical. **Prayer**. I recover back my divine gift by fire in the name of Jesus.

205. **IF YOU HARVEST WHEAT IN THE DREAM.** It is a sign of business or career fruitfulness. **Prayer**. I shall move forward by fire in the name of Jesus.

206. **IF YOU FALL INTO AN ENDLESS PIT IN THE DREAM.** It foretells doom in career or business. **Prayer**. O Lord lift me high above my enemies in the name of Jesus.

207. **IF YOUR PROPOSED LOVER GIVES YOU FLOWER IN THE DREAM.** It means approval and agreed love affair, **Prayer**. My marital moves shall not hit the rock in the name of Jesus.

208. **IF YOU EXPERIENCE FLOOD ATTACK IN THE DREAM.** It means strong danger and calamity is ahead of you. **Prayer.** Destruction that leads to sorrow in my life die by fire in the name of Jesus.

209. **IF YOU DESTROY YOUR VILLAGE SHRINE IN THE DREAM.** It means spiritual elevation against territorial powers in your environ. **Prayer.** Holy Ghost Fire, consume every power and principalities in charge of my environment in the name of Jesus.

210. **IF YOU SEE STRANGE WOMAN ON YOUR BED IN THE DREAM.** It means spirit woman that destroy marital home. **Prayer.** Any strange woman tormenting my marriage, die in the name of Jesus.

211. **IF YOU SEE POSTALS OF YOUR OBITUARY PASTED ON THE WALLS IN THE DREAM.** It signifies sudden death is programmed against you. **Prayer.** I release my spirit, soul and body from claws of untimely death in the name of Jesus.

212. **IF YOU HAVE A HANDSHAKE WITH A WITCH DOCTOR IN THE DREAM.** It is a sign of initiation into occult world. **Prayer.** I disassociate my life from evil gathering in the name of Jesus.

213. **IF YOU RUN ERRAND FOR PEOPLE IN THE DREAM.** It means spirit of slavery has taken over your life **Prayer**. My destiny shall not crawl in the name of Jesus.

214. **IF YOU ARE INVOLVED IN AN ENDLESS JOURNEY IN THE DREAM.** It means sweat without result. **Prayer**. I shall not dine with poverty in my life in the name of Jesus.

215. **IF YOU DREAM OF BARKING OF DOGS IN THE DREAM**. It means warning of attack of household wickedness **Prayer**. Holy Ghost Fire, disgrace every work of the wicked in my environment in the name of Jesus.

216. **IF YOU SING WORDLY SONGS IN THE DREAM.** It signifies distraction from the work of God. **Prayer**. Whatever may distract me from serving God die, in the name of Jesus.

217. **IF YOU PARTICIPATE IN A FOOTBALL MATCH IN THE DREAM.** It means you shall soon enter into contest in business or career. **Prayer.** Ability to excel with surprise fall upon me in the name of Jesus.

218. **IF YOU JOYFULLY COMPLETE A TASK IN THE DREAM.** It tells of greatness and fruitfulness awaiting you in your present venture. **Prayer**; Power that bring fruitfulness fall upon me, in the name of Jesus.

219. **IF YOU RECEIVE CROWN OF ADORATION IN THE DREAM.** It means promotion, advancement and leadership. **Prayer.** My head receive fulfillment of glory in the name of Jesus.

220. **IF YOUR TRAP CATCH ANIMALS IN THE DREAM.** It signifies fruitfulness in your business endeavour. **Prayer.** O Lord, transform my life for better in the name of Jesus.

221. **IF YOU SEE ASHES IN THE DREAM.** It means repentance. **Prayer.** O Lord, forgive me of my sins in the name of Jesus.

222. **IF YOU SEE ANIMALS EATING UP YOUR SEEDLINGS IN THE DREAM**. It means dark powers are planning to destroy your goodness at infancy. **Prayer**. 0 Lord blindfold my enemies as I progress in life in the name of Jesus.

223. **IF YOU SEE A NEWLY BUILT BRIDGE IN THE DREAM**. It means an in road to better opportunities that bring relief and blessings. **Prayer**. My lost opportunities gather yourself together and locate me by fire in the name of Jesus.

224. **IF YOU DREAM USING WALKING STICK IN THE DREAM.** It means you need a helping hand to progress. **Prayer**. My helper, locate me by fire in name of Jesus.

225. **IF YOU DREAM OF WITHDRAWING FROM YOUR BANK ACCOUNT**. It means financial loss in the physical is in the offing. **Prayer**. Every plan of the enemy to thwart my efforts shall fail in the name of Jesus.

226. **IF YOU LOSE OF SHEEP IN THE DREAM.** It means your spiritual efforts and leadership is under attack. **Prayer.** Every attack of the enemy to scatter my calling die in the name of Jesus.

227. **IF YOU SEE BRIGHT SUN SHINE IN THE DREAM.** It means open door to greatness and opportunities are in the offing. **Prayer.** Power to sow and reap fruits of my labour fall upon me in the name of Jesus.

228. **IF YOU CATCH FISH IN THE DREAM.** It means soul winning and improvement **Prayer.** O Lord give me spirit to excel in my calling in the name of Jesus.

229. **IF YOU CARRY FIREWOOD IN THE DREAM.** It means slavery. **Prayer.** O Lord, save me from physical and spiritual slavery in the name of Jesus.

230. **IF YOUR CLOTH IS MISSING IN THE DREAM.** It means emptiness and disgrace that leads to rejection and poverty. **Prayer.** Power of demotion in my life, die in the name of Jesus.

231. **IF YOU FIGHT AND YOUR AMMUNITION FINISH IN THE DREAM.** It signifies improper preparation in prayer or praying without zeal. **Prayer.** My Lord and my God envelope me with fresh fire in the name of Jesus.

232. **IF YOUR HOUSE IS OVERGROWN BY WEEDS IN THE DREAM.** It means powers of hindrance and failure has over power you. **Prayer.** Every effort of the enemy against my life meet double failure in the name of Jesus.

233. **IF YOU FIGHT AND KILL MAD MAN CHASING YOU IN THE DREAM.** It is victory over demonic powers assign against you **Prayer.** Every stubborn pursuer fashioned against my life die in the name of Jesus.

234. **IF YOUR TEETH IS BROKEN IN THE DREAM.** It means loss of strength in the physical. **Prayer.** My destiny, receive divine strength in the name of Jesus.

235. **IF YOUR BOAT CAPSIDE IN THE DREAM.** It means sudden failure in the midst of calm, business or career.

Prayer. Any power that wants to sow seed of sorrow in my joy die in the name of Jesus.

236. **IF A MOUNTAIN BEFORE YOU IN THE DREAM SUDDENLY DISAPPEAR**. It means victory after much prayers **Prayer**. Thou mountain of problems in my life disappear by fire, in the name of Jesus.

237. **IF YOU SEE A WELL FULL OF WATER IN THE DREAM**. It means abundance, peace of mind and blessings. **Prayer**. O Lord, surprise me with supernatural breakthrough in the name of Jesus.

238. **IF SUMMONED BEFORE OCCULT MEETING IN THE DREAM**. It means evil initiation or satanic judgment against your personality. **Prayer**. My spirit, refuse to obey evil judgment in the name of Jesus.

239. **IF YOU DREAM OF FALL AT THE EDGE OF BREAKTHROUGH**. It means that strong satanic decision has been taken against your prosperity. **Prayer**. I fire back every arrow of poverty against me in the name of Jesus.

240. **IF YOU STAND FACE TO FACE IN HOSTILITY WITH IDOL WORSHIPPERS IN THE DREAM.** It means you are under very strong curse. **Prayer**. My life, reject every captivity of spiritual wickedness in the name of Jesus.

241. **IF YOU DREAM AND SEE HEALTHY PALM TREE IN THE DREAM.** It means prosperity. **Prayer**. My breakthrough, appear by fire in the name of Jesus.

242. **IF INVOLVED IN AN ACCIDENT IN THE DREAM.** It means that serious disaster that may lead to untimely death is in the offing. **Prayer**. I break every backbone of untimely death in my life in the name of Jesus.

243. **IF YOU HAVE SEX WITH GOAT IN THE DREAM.** It means arrow of miserable life and diversion. **Prayer**. O Lord, destroy every power holding on to my blessings.

244. **IF A PIT IS DUGGED AND YOU ARE COMMAND TO ENTER IT IN THE DREAM.** It means disaster may arise from pursuits of spirit of death.

Prayer. Thou power digging my grave, enter it and bury yourself in the name of Jesus.

245. **IF SOMEONE COUNT YOUR MONEY AND DO AWAY WITH IT IN THE DREAM.** It means spiritual robber is assign against you. **Prayer.** Thou robbers in the dark be exposed and be disgraced, in the name of Jesus.

246. **IF YOU ARE OVERTAKEN BY LICE IN THE DREAM.** It means poverty or sickness. **Prayer.** Every spirit assign to cause poverty in my life die, in the name of Jesus.

247. **IF YOU ARE OFFERED TATTERED MAT IN THE DREAM.** It is a curse of poverty. **Prayer.** Thou earth open and swallow every spirit of poverty assign against me, in the name of Jesus.

248. **IF YOU ARE TRAILED BY UNKNOWN PERSON IN THE DREAM.** It means you have been labeled with evil mark of attraction for evil. **Prayer.** Blood of Jesus cleanse me of evil mark, in the name of Jesus.

249. **IF CHASED BY SNAKE IN THE DREAM.** It means strong serpentine

witchcraft attack to destroy your existence. **Prayer**. Any evil power delegated to kill me, kill yourself, in the name of Jesus.

250. **IF YOUR CERTIFICATE IS SMEARED WITH FAECES IN THE DREAM.** It is an arrow of failure and rejection. **Prayer**. Thou spirit of rejection in my life die, in the name of Jesus.

251. **IF YOU DREAM OF DIVERSE AFFLICTIONS.** It means sadness. **Prayer**. Riches and not sadness shall be my portion, in the name of Jesus.

252. **IF YOU ARE CHASED BY DOG IN THE DREAM.** It means confusion and disarray in business and calling. **Prayer**. Every power assigned to chase me out of my rightful position die by fire in the name of Jesus.

253. **IF YOUR MONEY IS SEIZED AND WASN'T RETURN TO YOU IN THE DREAM.** It means arrow of lack and failure is fired against you. **Prayer**. Every evil hand assign against my finance wither in the name of Jesus.

254. **IF YOU PLAY WITH SNAKES IN THE DREAM.** It means you have

serpentine covenant. **Prayer**. Every covenant I have with serpent spirit break in the name of Jesus.

255. **IF YOU ARE HARASSED WITH SEX IN THE DREAM**. It means spirit husband or spirit wife is after your life. **Prayer**. I break myself loose from every spirit husband or wife in the name of Jesus.

256. **IF YOU SUCCESSFULY DRAW WATER FROM THE WELL IN THE DREAM.** It means success and prosperity shall soon manifest in your life. **Prayer**. O Lord let me reap the fruit of my labour in the name of Jesus.

257. **IF YOU SUCCESSFULLY CLIMB LADDER IN THE DREAM.** It means you shall succeed in your present venture. **Prayer.** My breakthrough, appear by fire and remain permanent, in the name of Jesus.

258. **IF YOU HAVE SEX WITH DOG IN THE DREAM.** It means you are under serious arrest of fornication. **Prayer**. My spirit, refuse to bow to destruction in the name of Jesus.

259. **IF YOU CARRY EXCRETA IN THE DREAM.** It means pollution, rejection and poverty against your life. **Prayer.** I shall not be an experiment of failure in the hands of enemies in the name of Jesus.

260. **IF YOU ARE STABBED IN THE DREAM.** It is an arrow of sudden death. **Prayer**: I shall not die but live in the name of Jesus.

261. **IF YOU HAVE HEAVY EYEBROWS IN THE DREAM.** It means an upcoming period of distinction and success. **Prayer.** Every evil eye trailing me go blind in the name of Jesus.

262. **IF SURROUNDED BY STRANGE FACES THAT WANT TO ATTACK YOU IN THE DREAM.** These are witchcraft agents assign to destroy you. **Prayer**. My life, refuse satanic attack and be free by fire in the name of Jesus.

263. **IF YOU OPERATE A MACHINE AND IT BREAKS DOWN IN THE DREAM.** It means death of someone close to you or arrow of death is fired against you. **Prayer**. Thou negative

powers hunting me for death die, in the name of Jesus.

264. **IF YOU ARE PLACED BESIDE A GRAVE YARD IN THE DREAM.** It means death of someone close to you or arrow death is fired against you. **Prayer**. Thou negative powers hunting my life die, in the name of Jesus.

265. **IF YOU SEE COWRIES IN THE DREAM.** It means your virtues stolen by wicked powers shall be restored. **Prayer**. Holy Ghost Power restores unto me what enemies have stolen from me.

266. **IF YOU WRESTLE AND OVERPOWER MASQUERADE IN THE DREAM.** It means spiritual victory over ancestral power assign against you. **Prayer**. By fire by force my enemies shall surrender in the name of Jesus.

267. **IF YOU DREAM AND SEE GREEN VEGETATION IN THE DREAM.** It means good beginning that brings flourishes. **Prayer**. My good beginning shall bring good ending in the name of Jesus.

268. **IF A BIG TREE IS FELLED IN THE DREAM.** It means death of someone

important to you or yourself. **Prayer**. Thou arrow of death after my life go back to your sender in the name of Jesus.

269. **IF YOU SEE A CANDLE LIGHT GOING OUT IN THE DREAM:** It means your glory is dwindling seriously. **Prayer.** Every power of darkness delegated against my life clear away by fire.

270. **IF YOU SEE A VERY BIG EYE TRAILING YOU IN THE DREAM.** It means your glory is supervised by witchcraft eye. **Prayer.** Holy Ghost Fire break into pieces any evil mirror used in monitoring my life.   .

271. **IF CAT CHASED YOU IN THE DREAM.** It means. witchcraft pursuit that leads to disarray in life. **Prayer.** Holy Ghost Fire burn to ashes any witchcraft cat pursuing me for destruction in the name of Jesus.

272. **IF YOU SEE A LAMP GOING DEEM IN THE DREAM.** It means arrow of darkness has caught up with your glory. **Prayer.** O Lord save me

from attacks of darkness in the name of Jesus.

273. **IF YOU ROAM ABOUT IN THE MARKET IN THE DREAM**. It means slow or no progress at all in real life. **Prayer.** O Lord let me fulfill my destiny in the name of Jesus

274. **IF YOU SEE YOURSELF IN A MIRROR IN THE DREAM**. It means you shall soon experience spiritual and physical .loss. **Prayer.** Every contrary power after my life be defeated in the name of Jesus

275. **IF YOU SEE DRY WELL IN THE DREAM**. It means your efforts shall be fruitless. **Prayer.** Holy Ghost Power, save me from satanic captivity in the name of Jesus.

276. **IF YOU LOOK DOWN INTO A WELL AND SEE WATER FAR IN THE DREAM**. It means you shall exert effort in life before you can reap goodness. **Prayer.** 0 Lord catapult me to my goodness in the name of Jesus.

277. **IF YOU HOLD HOE IN THE DREAM**. It is a sign of strength towards your calling or business. **Prayer.** I shall

reap the fruit of my labour, in the name of Jesus.

278. **IF YOU DREAM OF A LANTERN WITH BRIGHT LIGHT**. It means your glory shall shine. **Prayer**. My star, receive resurrection power of God in the name of Jesus.

279. **IF YOU RECEIVE BIG YAM TUBER IN THE DREAM**. It means abundant blessing and riches are in the offing. **Prayer**. My Lord and my God bless me without delay in the name of Jesus.

280. **IF YOU RECEIVE BAD YAM TUBERS IN THE DREAM**. It means poverty and sorrow in the offing. **Prayer**. My Lord and my God open new doors for me in the name of Jesus

281. **IF YOU SUCCESSFULLY CLIMB STAIRCASE IN THE DREAM.** It means victory and success; **Prayer**, 0 Lord open unto me all closed doors of prosperity in the name of Jesus

282. **IF YOU BEAT DRUM IN THE DREAM**. It means many are willing to serve you well. **Prayer**. O Lord let every trace of leadership m me manifest by fire in the name of Jesus.

283. **IF YOU SKETCH OR DRAW IN THE DREAM.** It means you shall experience slowness in progress and satanic delay in life. **Prayer.** Every power of delay fashion against my progress die in the name of Jesus.

284. **IF YOU DREAM THAT YOUR WRISTWATCH IS IN PERFECT WORKING ORDER.** It means that your time to answered prayer is at hand. **Prayer.** My time thou shall not pass me by in the name of Jesus.

285. **IF YOUR HEAD IS ANOINTED WITH OIL IN THE DREAM.** This is sign of ministerial calling. **Prayer.** Call of God fall upon me in the name of Jesus.

286. **IF YOU WALK ABOUT IN THE DESERT IN THE DREAM.** It means you are under arrest of spirit of desert and loneliness. **Prayer.** Every power connecting me to marine agent die in the name of Jesus.

287. **IF YOU SEE A DRY TREE IN THE DREAM.** It means arrow of failure is in the offing. **Prayer.** Thou spirit of failure

targeted against my life backfire, in the name of Jesus.

288. **IF YOU SEE AN UNCOMPLETED ROAD IN THE DREAM.** It means that your breakthrough needs urgent attention to come to pass. **Prayer.** O Lord open new ways of blessings unto my life in the name of Jesus.

289. **IF YOU SEE BIRD ON YOUR WINDOW GLARING AT YOU IN THE DREAM.** This is a witchcraft monitoring power. **Prayer.** Any evil bird assign to monitor my life be roasted to ashes, in the name of Jesus.

290. **IF YOU ARE ABOUT TO WED AND DREAM OF WOULD BE SPOUSE RECEIVING YOUR WEDDING RING** It means a divine revelation. **Prayer.** 0 Lord, reveal my life partner to me, in the name of Jesus.

291. **IF WRITING AND YOUR HAND OR BOOK GOT STAINED.** It means you can be implicated unjustly. **Prayer.** Any power behind my downfall, die, in the name of Jesus.

292. **IF YOU CARRY POT ON YOUR HEAD IN THE DREAM.** It 'means that

enemies have finalize their destructive plans against you. **Prayer.** 'Owner of evil load carry your load in the name of Jesus.

293. **IF YOUR NECK IS SQUEEZED AND COUL.D NOT FIGHT BACK IN THE DREAM.** It means there is witchcraft attack against your life that may cause untimely death or delay in progress. **Prayer.** Thou evil hand, assign to destroy me wither in the name of Jesus.

294. **IF YOU DRINK POISON IN THE DREAM.** It means satanic agenda of untimely death awaits you .**Prayer.** My life, refuse evil manipulation in the name of Jesus.

295. **IF YOU LOOK TIRED IN THE DREAM.** It means fruitless labour and spiritual slavery. **Prayer.** Every power, using me for satanic forced labour die, in the name of Jesus.

296. **IF YOU SEE GREAT GULLY IN THE DREAM.** It means existence of an obstacle between you and your success. **Prayer.** Every obstacle hindering my success in life disappear by fire In the name of Jesus

297. **IF YOUR WEDDING GOWN IS TORN IN THE DREAM.** It means marital arrow is fired to scatter your marriage. **Prayer.** Any power delegated to scatter my marriage die in the name of Jesus.

298. **IF YOU ARE NAKED IN THE MARKET IN THE DREAM.** It means you shall experience business failure. **Prayer.** Any power, feeding me with poverty, die in the name of Jesus.

299. **IF YOU HEAR GINGLE OF PRAYER BELL IN THE DREAM.** It means good news. **Prayer.** Thou fruit of my labour appear by fire and locate me in the name of Jesus.

300. **IF YOUR BABY BREAK YOUR T.V. SET IN THE DREAM.** It means your position and seriousness with your creator is shaking .**Prayer.** I break myself loose from strongholds of spiritual barrenness in the name of Jesus.

301. **IF YOU WAIL AND COMPLAIN BITTERLY IN THE DREAM.** It means arrow of confusion and satanic attack. **Prayer.** Every arrow of confusion

fired against my life backfire by fire, in the name of Jesus.

302. **IF YOU ARE ABOUT TO BOARD AIRCRAFT BUT SAW STRANGE PEOPLE IN BLACK DRESS AROUND YOU**. It means evil monitoring power is assign against you. **Prayer.** I command every power assign to monitor me for evil to roast by fire in the name of Jesus

303. **IF STRANGE HAND IS LAID ON YOUR HEAD IN THE DREAM.** It means evil initiation and attack. **Prayer.** My glory, refuse to cooperate with enemies in the name of Jesus.

304. **IF YOU ARE ANOINTED IN THE DREAM BY A GRAY HAIR PERSON**. It means authority and spiritual elevation .**Prayer.** Fresh anointing of the Living God fall upon me in the name of Jesus. .

305. **IF YOU MENSTRUATE IN THE DREAM** It means danger of miscarriage on the way. **Prayer.** I refuse to bury my baby In the Spirit in the name of Jesus.

306. **IF YOU SEE PIG IN THE DREAM.** It means rejection and dishonour, **Prayer.**

Satan, you shall not rubbish my honour and glory in the name of Jesus.   .

307. **IF YOU HAVE BABIES IN THE DREAM.** It means problems and inability to have issues in the physical. **Prayer.** Every strange children in my life die in the name of Jesus.

308. **IF YOU DREAM OF CHURCH CURTAIN TORE TO PIECES.** It means disunity among members and pastors. **Prayer.** Every arrow of disunity back fire in the name of Jesus.

309. **IF YOU CARRY BRAND NEW BAG IN THE DREAM.** It means prosperity and riches. **Prayer.** O Lord let my heart desire locate me by fire, in the name of Jesus.

310. **IF YOU HARVEST PEPPER IN THE DREAM.** It means affliction in the offing. **Prayer.** My spirit, soul and body refuse to co-operate with poverty, in the name of Jesus.

311. **IF PURSUED AND YOUR LEG BREAK IN THE DREAM.** I t means enemies have succeeded in firing arrow of delay into your life. **Prayer.** Any

power assign to trouble my Israel be troubled in the name of Jesus.

312. **IF YOU HOLD GUN IN THE DREAM.** It means spiritual power. **Prayer.** I shall not fall in my spiritual race in the name of Jesus.

313. **IF YOU RECEIVE SWORD IN THE DREAM.** It denotes victory and spiritual elevation. **Prayer.** Every Goliath on my way I cut you down with sword of God, in the name of Jesus.

314. **IF YOU SEE PEPPER IN THE DREAM.** It is a sign of misfortune and miscarriage. **Prayer.** Every power assign to sow poverty in my life, die in the name of Jesus.

315. **IF YOU SEE WIRLD WIND IN THE DREAM.** It means confusion that leads to destruction. **Prayer.** My father and my God remove every embargo on my way in the name of Jesus.

316. **IF YOU DREAM THAT YOUR PROPERTY WENT IN FLAME IN THE DREAM.** It means great care is needed on whatever you lay your hand upon to avoid disaster in the physical.

Prayer. Thou power of disaster against my life die in the name of Jesus.

317. **IF YOU SEE A LAME HIDING HIS FACE AS MUCH AS YOU WANT TO IDENTIFY HIM IN THE DREAM**. It is you in the physical. You have backslid. **Prayer** Blood of Jesus cleanse me of filth holding me in bondage

318. **IF YOU SEE A BLACK GOAT EATING BEFORE YOU IN THE DREAM.** It means your blessings is been consumed by witchcraft powers. **Prayer.** Any power assign to eat my blessings eat yourself, in the name of Jesus.

319. **IF YOU DREAM OF MULTIPLE DEATH OF BOTH OLD AND YOUNG**. It means sudden uproar in the offing. **Prayer.** Agent of death in my vicinity, die by fire in the name of Jesus.

320. **IF YOU ARE IN A DARK VALLEY IN THE DREAM.** It means wicked spiritual arrest and stagnation. **Prayer.** 0 Lord give me divine wisdom over poverty in the name of Jesus.

321. **IF YOUR BODY IS FULL OF WOUND IN THE DREAM**. It means arrow of affliction and untimely death. **Prayer.** Any power assign to kill me kill yourself and die, in the name of Jesus.

322. **IF YOU ARE INVOLVED IN AN ACCIDENT IN THE DREAM.** It means serious household wickedness in your life. **Prayer.** O Lord, save me from evil hand in the name of Jesus.

323. **IF YOU SEE AN ANIMAL TIED TO A PARTICULAR SPOT IN THE DREAM.** It means you have been tied to a spot spiritually. **Prayer**. Any evil rope used in tying me down break by fire in the name of Jesus.

324. **IF YOU BOLDLY HOLD CUTLASS IN YOUR HAND IN THE DREAM**. It means spiritual strength and 'power. **Prayer.** o Lord empower me to overcome and conquer In the name of Jesus:

325. **IF YOU FIND YOURSELF IN A DEEP PIT BUT COULD NOT GET OUT BEFORE YOU WAKE UP.** It means captivity and arrow of delay, **Prayer.** Holy Ghost Power free me from

every satanic capacity in the name of Jesus.

326. **IF YOU SEE POLICE CHECK POINT IN THE DREAM.** It means organized power assigned against your moving forward. **Prayer.** Every satanic road block holding me back scatter by fire in the name of Jesus.

327. **IF YOU SEE YOURSELF IN YOUR VILLAGE IN THE DREAM.** It means demotion and backwardness. **Prayer.** Any spirit of backwardness delegated against me die in the name of Jesus.

328. **IF YOU ARE WITH YOUR PLAY MATES IN THE BEACH IN THE DREAM.** It means relationship with marine agents. **Prayer.** Every power connecting me to marine agent die in the name of Jesus.

329. **IF YOU ARE GIVEN FRESH FRUIT IN THE DREAM.** It means prosperity and divine intervention, to breakthrough. **Prayer.** My open heaven appear today in the name of Jesus.

330. **IF YOU SEE OKRO OR PLUCK IT IN THE DREAM.** It means

sluggishness and procrastination on your side. **Prayer**. Every arrow of sluggishness fired against my life back fire in the name of Jesus.

331. **IF YOU EXPERIENCE FLOOD IN THE DREAM.** It means untimely death, or failure in business that can lead to suicide. **Prayer**. I refuse to swim in the ocean of poverty in the name of Jesus.

332. **IF YOU SLEEP IN THE CEMETARY IN THE DREAM**. It means untimely death is knocking at your door or someone close to you. **Prayer.** Thou spirit of death after my life die in the name of Jesus.

333. **IF OFFERED EGG IN THE DREAM.** It means opportunities that will transform your life is in the offing. **Prayer**. My joy appear today and forever more in the name of Jesus.

334. **IF YOU FLY IN THE DREAM**. It means witchcraft possession. **Prayer.** Every witchcraft power, assign to dominate my life break in the name of Jesus.

335. **IF YOU SEE A FULL BRIGHT MOON IN THE DREAM**. It means

your glory shall shine and people shall serve you **Prayer.** My star, arise and shine in the name of Jesus.   .

336. **IF YOU EAT IN THE CEMETARY IN THE DREAM.** It means your life is hunted by spirit of death. **Prayer.** My life, refuse to be captivated by spirit of untimely death in the name of Jesus.

337. **IF YOUR BUCKET FALL HALF WAY AS YOU FETCH WATER FROM A WELL IN THE DREAM.** It means your present venture is good but strong attack awaits to cut it short. **Prayer.** Any power, assign to bury my joy, die in the name of Jesus.

338. **IF YOU SEE DAMAGED EYES IN THE DREAM.** It means sickness and spiritual blindness. **Prayer,** Every captivity of sickness and spiritual loss in my life break in the name of Jesus.

339. **IF YOU SEE HORSE IN THE DREAM.** It means long life and rest of mind. **Prayer.** My joy to serve the Lord shall bring me success and long life in the name of Jesus.

340. **IF YOU HEAR SOUNDS OF DRUM IN YOUR DREAM.** It means that

fortune shall find and locate you from diverse directions. **Prayer.** Abundance of wealth in the order of Obededum, locate me by fire in the name of Jesus.

341. **IF PREGNANT AND PURSUED BY MASQUERADE IN THE DREAM**. This is a serious attack against save delivery. **Prayer.** Every effort of wicked powers against my life, die in the name of Jesus.

342. **IF YOU DIG FORTUNES IN A BURIAL GROUND IN THE DREAM**. It means you will soon experience breakthrough that was stolen by the wicked that are dead. **Prayer.** Every arrow of poverty against my life backfire in the name of Jesus:

343. **IF YOU VOMIT WORM IN THE DREAM**. It means victory over satanic deposit in your life. **Prayer.** Every evil plantation in my life die in the name of Jesus.

344. **IF YOU HOLD HOOK BY A RIVER OR POND BUT NEVER USE IT IN THE DREAM**. It means arrow of ministerial confusion and emptiness.

Prayer. Every curse of poverty placing me in bondage break in the name

345. **IF PREGNANT AND PURSUED BY COW IN THE DREAM.** It means wicked powers that cause miscarriage is after your life. **Prayer.** My destiny fulfill divine fruitfulness, in the name of Jesus,

346. **IF YOU FIGHT MASQUERADE IN THE DREAM.** It means spiritual warfare. **Prayer.** Any power assign to destroy my destiny die, in the name of Jesus.

347. **IF YOU SEE CANDLE LIGHT UNDER A BUSHEL IN THE DREAM.** It means self-destruction. **Prayer.** Every step that I shall take that will lead to self-destruction be cancelled, in the name of Jesus.

348. **IF YOU ARE LIFTED HIGH IN BLACK BIRD'S WING IN THE DREAM.** It means you have been satanically initiated to carry out evil. **Prayer.** I break every initiation I have with evil powers, in the name of Jesus.

349. **IF YOU SUCCESSFULLY CROSS A BRIDGE IN THE DREAM.** It means you shall experience breakthrough in

your undertaking. **Prayer.** 1 shall succeed in the name of Jesus.

350. **IF YOU DREAM AND SEE A DRY WELL IN THE DREAM.** It means manifestation of poverty in the offing. **Prayer.** My life, shall not associate with poverty, in the name of Jesus.   .

351. **IF YOU SEE A COMPLETED NEW BUILDING IN YOUR DREAM.** It means open heaven towards success in life. **Prayer.** O heaven cooperate with me for success and excellence in the name of Jesus.

352. **IF YOU CLIMB MOUNTAIN WITH DIFFICULTY IN THE DREAM.** It means enemies have overtaken you, you may sow but difficult to harvest the fruit of your labour. **Prayer.** O Lord bless my handwork, in the name of Jesus.

353. **IF YOU SEE SPROUT OF A TREE COVERED BY BEES IN THE DREAM.** It means there is an attack against your star from youth. **Prayer.** My star arise and shine, in the name of Jesus.

354. **IF SMOKE OVERTAKES YOU IN THE KITCHEN IN THE DREAM.** It means affliction and rebellion is

fashioned against your joy **Prayer.** My laughter shall not be caught short by powers of darkness, in the name of Jesus.

355. **IF YOU DREAM OF PALM OIL BOTTLE**. It means comfort and happiness. **Prayer.** I claim my possessions by fire in the name of Jesus.

356. **IF YOU DREAM OF GARDEN FULL OF FRESH AND ROBUST GARDEN EGGS**. It means success and prosperity. **Prayer.** 0 Lord let success and prosperity locate me by fire in the name of Jesus.

357. **IF YOU DREAM OF STRANGE PEOPLE HOLDING MEETING IN THE CHURCH ALTAR.** It means satanic representatives have taken over the church to fire satanic arrows. **Prayer.** God of Elijah, scatter every evil gathering against my life in the name of Jesus.

358. **IF YOU HAVE SEX WITH COW IN THE DREAM.** It means you may experience confusion in your undertaking. **Prayer.** 0 Lord let disgrace and defeat be far from me in my life in the name of Jesus.

359. **IF INCISION IS MADE IN YOUR BODY IN THE DREAM**. It means initiation into dark powers, loss of memory and ill luck **Prayer**. My father and my God, make my life too hot for enemies to handle in the name of Jesus.

360. **IF YOU PICK SNAILS IN THE DREAM.** It means delay and slow progress in life. **Prayer.** Spirit of snail in my life die in the name of Jesus.

361. **IF YOU SING FUNERAL SONGS IN THE DREAM.** It is a sign of untimely death. **Prayer.** Every arrow of death fired against me backfire in the name of Jesus.

362. **IF WET BY RAIN IN THE DREAM**. It means trouble is awaiting you. **Prayer.** Evil rains that shower to disgrace me stop, in the name of Jesus.

363. **IF YOUR CERTIFICATE IS STOLEN IN THE DREAM**. It is satanic attack that leads to unemployment or loss of contract. **Prayer.** Fire of the Holy Ghost locate and return my certificates to me by fire in the name of Jesus.

364. **IF YOU SEE DOG IN THE DREAM.** It means lust to sexual appetite. **Prayer.**

Fire of God; consume every appetite for loss of flesh in my life in the name of Jesus.

365. **IF YOU ARE GIVEN HOT PURSUIT IN THE DREAM.** It means stubborn pursuers are after your life. **Prayer**. Every stubborn pursuer after my life fall down and die in the name of Jesus.

YOU HAVE BATTLES TO WIN
TRY THESE BOOKS
1. COMMAND THE DAY

Each day of the week is loaded with meanings and divine assurance. God did not create each day of the week for the fun of it. Blessings, success, gifts, resources, hopes, portfolios, duties, rights, prophecies, warnings and challenges, are loaded in each day.

Do you know the language, command or decree you can use to claim what belongs to you in each day of the week? Do you know in Christendom, Monday can be equated to one of the days of creation in Genesis chapter one? Do you know creation lasted for six days and God rested on the seventh day? What day of the week can Christian equate as the first day of the week, if we follow Christian calendar? What day can we call day seven?

This book shall give insight to these questions. It shall explain how you can command each day of the week according to creation in the book of Genesis chapter one.

Above all, you shall exercise your right and claim what is hidden in each day of the week.

Check for this in *COMMAND THE DAY.*

2. PRAYER TO REMEMBER DREAMS

A lot of people are passing through this spiritual epidemic on a daily basis. Their dream life is epileptic, having no ability to remember all dreams they dream, or sometimes forget everything entirely. This is nothing but spiritual havoc you need to erase from your spiritual record.

The answer to every form of spiritual blackout caused by spiritual erasers is found in, *PRAYER TO REMEMBER DREAMS.*

3.100% CONFESSSIONS AND PROPHECIES TO LOCATE HELPERS.

This is a wonderful book on confessions and prophecies to locate helpers and helpers to locate you. It is a prayer book loaded with over two thousand (2,000) prayer points.

The book unravels how to locate unknown helpers, prayers to arrest mind of helpers and prayers for manifestation after encounter with helpers.

4. ANOINTING FOR ELEVENTH HOUR HELP.

This book tells much of what to do at injury hour called eleventh hour. When you read and use this book as prescribed fear shall vanish in your life when pursuing a project, career or contract.

5. PRAYER TO LOCATE HELPERS.

Our divine helper is God. He created us to be together and be of help to one another. In the midst of no help we lost out, ending our journey in the wilderness.

There are keys assign to open right doors of life. You need right key to locate your helpers. Enough is enough; of suffering in silence.

With this book, you shall locate your helpers while your helpers shall locate you.

6. FIRE FOR FIRE PRAYER BOOK

This prayer book is fast at answering spiritual problems. It is a bulldozer prayer book, full of prayers all through. It is highly recommended for night vigil. Testimonies are pouring in daily from users of this book across the world!

7. PRAYER FOR THE FRUIT OF THE WOMB

This prayer book is children magnet. By faith and believe in God Almighty, as soon as you use this book open doors to child bearing shall be yours. Amen

8. PRAYER FOR PREGNANT WOMEN.

This is a spiritual prayer book loaded with prayers of solution for pregnant women. As soon as you take in, the prayers you shall pray from day one of conception to the day of delivery are written in this book.

9. WARFARE IN THE OFFICE

It is high time you pray prayers of power must change hands in office. Use this book and liberate yourself from every form of office yoke.

10. MY MARRIAGE SHALL NOT BREAK

Marriage is corner piece of life, happiness and joy. You need to hold it tight and guide it from wicked intruders and destroyer of homes.

11. VICTORY OVER SATANIC HOUSE part 1&2

Are you a tenant, Land lord bombarded left and right, front and back by wicked people around you?

With this book you shall be liberated from the hooks of the enemy.

12. DICTIONARY OF DREAMS

This is a must book for every home. It gives accurate details to about **10,000 (Ten thousand) dreams and interpretations,** written in alphabetical order for quick reference and easy digestion. The book portrays spiritual revelations with sound prophetic guidelines. It is loaded with Biblical references and violent prayers.

Ask for yours today.

For Further Enquiries Contact
THE AUTHOR
EVANGELIST TELLA OLAYERI
P.O. Box 1872 Shomolu Lagos.
Tel: 08023583168

FROM AUTHOR'S DESK

BEFORE YOU GO

Hello,

Thank you for purchasing this book. Would you consider posting a review about this book? In addition to providing feedback and arousing others into Christ's bosom, reviews can help other customers to know about the book.

Please take a minute to leave a review on this book, no matter how short it is.

I would appreciate that!

Thank you in advance, for your review and your patronage!!

NOTE: You can get all my books from my website www.tellaolayeri.com

GOOD NEWS!!!

My audiobook is now available. To get one go to acx.com and search **Tella Olayeri**.

Thanks.

Made in the USA
Las Vegas, NV
24 October 2024

10395038R00056